Published by
*Federation of Family
History Societies
(Publications) Ltd.*
2-4 Killer Street,
Ramsbottom, Bury,
Lancashire BL0 9BZ,
United Kingdom

Copyright © Audrey Collins

ISBN 1-86006-090-0

First published 1998

Printed and bound by
Oxuniprint
Great Clarendon Street
Oxford OX2 6DP

Basic

Using W

First Avenue House

Audrey Collins

SERIES EDITOR
Pauline M. Litton

FEDERATION OF FAMILY HISTORY SOCIETIES

CONTENTS

Getting There: Map	2
Introduction	3
Getting There (First Avenue House)	3
Facilities at First Avenue House	4
Principal Registry of the Family Division (PRFD)	4
Wills and Administrations	5
Grants of Representation	5
The Contents of Wills	7
Intestacy	11
Searching in the Indexes	12
Reading and Copying	13
Orders by Post	15
Useful Addresses	16
Bibliography	16

FIRST AVENUE HOUSE

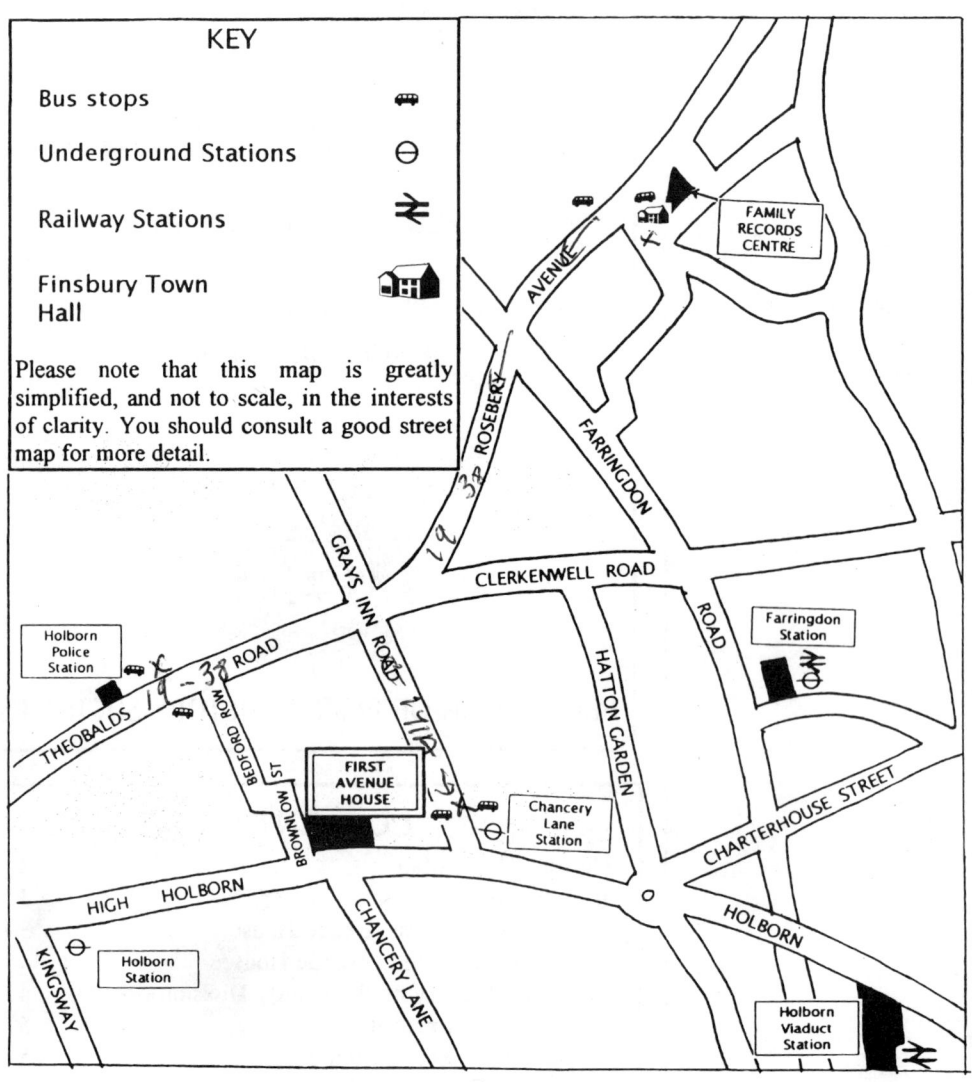

INTRODUCTION

Somerset House has closed its doors to the genealogist for the last time. Until 1974 this was the place to go for birth, marriage and death certificates; even now some people still go there first, so ingrained is the name 'Somerset House' in the national consciousness. Until May 1998, it was the place to look for wills and letters of administration from 1858 onwards, in the custody of the Principal Registry of the Family Division. In June 1998, the Principal Registry opened for business in its new home, First Avenue House, High Holborn, premises formerly occupied by HMSO Bookshop.

The purpose of this guide is to describe the records now held at First Avenue House, the means of access to them, and their use to the family historian. It also deals with some records and indexes elsewhere, and applications by post.

Principal Registry of the Family Division
Probate Department
First Avenue House
42-49 High Holborn
London WC1V 6NP   Phone: 0171-936 7000

Opening Hours: 10.00am - 4.30pm, Monday to Friday
Closed weekends and Bank Holidays

GETTING THERE

First Avenue House is situated on the north side of High Holborn, midway between Chancery Lane and Holborn underground stations, and is on several bus routes. Both of the Underground stations are on the Central Line, and Holborn is also on the Piccadilly Line. The nearest railway stations are Farringdon and Holborn Viaduct. Buses which travel along High Holborn are: 8, which runs between Victoria and Bow, via Liverpool Street; 22b, Tottenham Court Road to Homerton, via Liverpool Street; 25, Oxford Circus to Ilford; 501 and 521, between Waterloo and London Bridge. From the Family Records Centre in Myddelton Street, the best route is to take any bus from Finsbury Town Hall. If you take the 171a, you should alight at the southern end of Grays Inn Road. The 19 and 38 buses take a different route, along Theobalds Road, and the stop you need is opposite Holborn Police Station. This is a request stop, so you should ask the conductor to tell you when you get there. From either of these stops it is only a short walk to First Avenue House. If you are making the journey back to the Family Records Centre by bus, it is best to take the 19 or 38. Not only do you have a choice of two buses, but they are both more frequent than the 171a. If you choose to walk from the Family Records Centre, it takes about 20 minutes (see map).

Facilities at First Avenue House

Facilities for visitors to First Avenue House are better than they were at Somerset House. There are plenty of cafés, pubs and sandwich bars in the surrounding area, as well as shops, banks and cash dispensers. The entrance to the building is at the corner of High Holborn and Brownlow Street. On entering, you must pass through a security barrier, where all bags are X-rayed. The Probate Department is clearly signposted to your left. Eating and drinking are not permitted in the search room, but you will see a seating area just before the entrance to it, where you may have your lunch or a drink. Lockers where you can leave bags and luggage have been promised, but at the time of writing had still not arrived. There are also toilets and payphones. Follow the signs for the enquiry desk in the main foyer, and you will see them signposted ahead of you.

Inside the search room, you will find that it is light and spacious, with plenty of seating. In Somerset House, personal applications from executors of the recently deceased were dealt with on a separate floor, but here they share the same search room and cashier's window with the indexes. The first thing you will see on entering the search room is the waiting area and enquiry desk for these personal applications. To your left is the rest of the search room where you may consult the indexes, and read copies of wills. The earlier indexes, 1858 to 1943, are to the left, and 1944 onwards on the right. There are eight microfiche readers for searching the most recent indexes, an enquiry desk, and the cashier's window. In the centre of the room are several tables, and there is additional seating around the room.

PRINCIPAL REGISTRY OF THE FAMILY DIVISION (PRFD)

This is part of the Court Service, and was formerly known as the Principal Probate Registry, which holds a copy of every Grant of Representation in England and Wales from 12th January 1858 to the present day. This is the document required by the executors or administrators to collect in and distribute the estate of a deceased person. It will be a Grant of Probate if that person left a will, and a Grant of Letters of Administration if they did not. The PRFD also holds a copy of all the wills for which a Grant of Probate has been issued. When a Grant of Probate is made, the will is said to have been proved. Letters of Administration are often referred to as admons. The system which came into effect in 1858, following the Probate Act of 1857, replaced one where matters of probate were dealt with by a variety of church courts. For more information on the situation before 1858, you should consult Jane Cox's *Introduction to Wills Probate & Death Duty Records; Affection Defying the Power of Death.* Although the family historian will be interested mainly in the wills and administrations left by ancestors many years ago, looking after these is only part of the PRFD's work. Much of their time is spent dealing with applications for grants of probate and administration from the executors or next of kin of the recently deceased. Nowadays a far higher proportion of people leave a will than, say, a century ago, and the population itself is of course much larger than it was. The PRFD has to keep registered copies of all these documents, which in recent years has led to major storage problems. This was one of the reasons the wills and administrations were moved to a separate location, while the indexes were still at their former home, Somerset House. Unfortunately there is no prospect that the wills and indexes will be reunited on one site in the foreseeable future. There are also District Probate Registries and Sub-Registries around England and Wales, where executors and administrators can apply for their Grants. Some of them have copies of the national indexes, though not necessarily for all years from 1858. Copies of the wills proved at a District Registry may also be held there, but many have been deposited in County Record Offices. Sub-Registries are generally smaller than District Registries, and may not have search facilities. For the addresses of District Registries, Sub-Registries and details of their holdings, you should consult the latest edition of Jeremy Gibson's **Probate Jurisdictions: Where To Look For Wills**, or the **Genealogical Services Directory**.

WILLS AND ADMINISTRATIONS

Grants of Representation

A will is a legal document in which a person leaves instructions for the distribution of their property, called the estate, after their death. The person making a will is called the testator, or testatrix if female. The will must be in writing, signed by the testator, and witnessed by two people who are not going to benefit from it. It should also name at least one executor. A female executor is an executrix. It is the duty of the executors to carry out the wishes of the testator, as expressed in the will. To do this, the executors must apply for a Grant of Probate. Banks and other institutions require this before they will release funds, deeds of property and so on. If no will can be found, then interested parties, usually the family of the deceased, may apply for a Grant of Letters of Administration. It may also be necessary to apply for a Grant of Letters of Administration when a valid will exists, but the executor or executors named in it are unwilling or unable to carry out their duties. There are, then, three possible outcomes, probate, administration, or administration (with will annexed). Once probate or administration has been granted, brief details will appear in the index volume for the year in which the grant was made. This will usually be the same as the year of death, but may be the following year, or even later in some cases. Where probate or administration with will annexed has been granted, you will be able to order the will and the grant, but in the case of administration, there is only the grant.

Who made wills?

In the first years after 1858, only a minority of people left wills, or assets for which administration was needed. For a variety of reasons the proportion has steadily increased since then. In the 19th century, most testators were men, since the property of a married woman belonged in law to her husband, unless it had been specifically designated for her own personal use, under the terms of a marriage settlement or perhaps her father's will. See 'Women and Wills', below, for more detail. They were therefore not entitled to make wills, though some did, with their husband's permission, often for the distribution of personal items such as jewellery. Some wealthy wives also had property of their own as a result of marriage settlements. Following the Married Women's Property Act of 1882, women who married after that date could make wills in their own right. Spinsters and widows had always been entitled to make wills, assuming they had anything to leave. Testators also had to be 21 or over, except in the case of soldiers and sailors on active service. You might assume that only the well-off left a will, and it is not worth looking for wills if your ancestors were labourers or artisans. This is not necessarily the case. Although most people of this sort did not leave a will, some did, and in the years when the indexes show the occupations of testators, you will see labourers, railway porters and factory workers among the farmers, merchants and doctors. An ancestor who was in the Army or Navy might have made a will, leaving his few possessions to his nearest and dearest, or his mother or widow might have needed to apply for letters of administration to collect his back pay.

Scotland, Ireland and overseas

Some wills relate to people who died outside England and Wales, and whose death entry will not be found in the Civil Registration death indexes at the Family Records Centre. These will include members of the Armed Forces, and those who lived and worked abroad, but retained property in England and Wales, as well as some who died overseas while on a short visit. Scotland and Ireland have their own legal systems and arrangements for probate. If a Scottish or Irish person had property in England, you might find their will proved in the PRFD, but if the terms 'confirmed' or 'sealed' appear in the index, the will was proved in Scotland or Ireland, and the only record of this at the PRFD is a document similar to a Grant, containing little or no information which does not appear in the index. Scottish wills are in the Scottish Record Office and Irish ones in the National Archives in Dublin, except for Northern Ireland wills after

1918, which are in the Public Record Office of Northern Ireland in Belfast. Many Irish wills were destroyed when the National Archives in Dublin, then known as the Public Record Office, was burned down in 1922. The term 'sealed' may also apply to the wills of residents of other parts of the British Empire, later the Commonwealth. Wills and administrations of the British in India can be found in the Oriental and India Office Collections of the British Library.

People who did not leave wills

By contrast with the unexpected finding of wills left by labourers and the like, there are cases where you might expect to find a will, but do not. You may know from other research that your ancestor was comfortably-off, and be surprised to find no will or administration for him or her. Apart from those cases where probate was not granted until many years after the death, there are several possible reasons for this. First of all, it may be that the person concerned did not actually own the capital from which their income was derived, but only had a life interest in it, perhaps under the terms of the earlier will of a father or husband. Secondly, they may have been clever enough to make over their property to their heirs well before they died, in such a way as to avoid death duties. Remember that a grant of probate would be needed to gain access to a bank account or other investments in a person's name, but if all their assets were in the form of cash or moveable goods, then there would be no need to go to the trouble and expense of legal proceedings.

When wills were made

In most cases, testators did not make a will until shortly before they died, as will be apparent from the date of the will and the subsequent date of death. Some people, however, made wills much earlier, sometimes around the time of their marriage, or during a serious illness, or soon after receiving an inheritance themselves. If the person then lived for some time after this will was made, they had plenty of time to change their mind about its contents, or they might feel the need to alter it in the light of changed circumstances. One or more of the intended beneficiaries might have died, and others could have fallen in or out of favour. If the change was a small one, rather than write a completely new will, the testator might make an addition called a codicil. This had to be dated, signed and witnessed in the same way as the will, and appears after the end of it. If a will has a codicil, this will be indicated in the index.

The contents of wills

Many of the phrases found in wills are standard legal terms, which can look intimidating, but, with practice, you can learn to recognize them. They may be lengthy, and appear unnecessarily complicated, but often they are used so as to make the terms of the will absolutely unambiguous. Common English may work very well in ordinary conversation, but it is not always the clearest form of expression in a legal document. You need not dwell on these standard phrases, but can move on to the parts of the will which are of most interest to the family historian, that is, the family information. Most wills start with 'This is the last will and testament of ...'. Strictly speaking, a will deals with real estate, ie land and buildings, while a testament is for personal estate, which is money and moveable property, such as jewellery and furniture. In practice, the use of this phrase at the start of a will has no real significance in the period after 1858. The phrase 'I hereby revoke all former wills' or its equivalent, may also appear. This is not strictly necessary, since a valid will automatically supersedes any previous one. If a person married, any will they had already made became invalid, unless it had been made with the impending marriage in mind, and said so. The testator will also appoint executors, and there will usually be an instruction to the executors to pay any debts and funeral expenses. Occasionally there will be specific instructions as to burial or cremation. Finally, the testator will arrive at the main purpose of the will, which is to give details of who is to receive what from the estate.

Executors

In many cases, a testator will appoint as executors members of his own family, often his wife. An executor may turn out be a relative, even if this is not specifically stated in the will. An executor may also be a beneficiary of the will and in many cases is the main, or even the only, beneficiary. If a testator's wife is described in the index as 'widow and relict' then this means that she inherits everything. If the will makes provision for ongoing payments, such as an income for life for a widow, or for the upkeep of children until they come of age, the testator will also name trustees, usually the executors, to see that this is done. Sometimes the executor is a solicitor, or even a bank, acting in a professional capacity for the testator.

Bequests and legacies

These are the terms used to describe anything a testator leaves in a will. The recipients are called beneficiaries, or legatees. If someone is a 'universal legatee' they inherit all the testator's estate; if a residuary legatee they inherit anything left after the other specific bequests have been made. Bequests may be 'absolute' or 'conditional'. Anything left absolutely becomes the beneficiary's property, for them to do with as they please. A conditional bequest is where the beneficiary only inherits if certain conditions are fulfilled. This could be an annual income paid to a man's widow unless or until she re-marries, or a sum paid to one of his children on condition that he or she looks after another member of the family, who is perhaps an invalid. Legacies were sometimes left to servants, on condition that they were still in the testator's employment at the time of his or her decease. A bequest may also be 'in trust', usually until one of the beneficiaries comes of age, or marries. In this case, the testator will appoint a trustee or trustees, often the same people as the executors, to carry out this duty, a responsibility which could last for many years.

Family information from wills

The obvious information you will find in a will is when a testator names members of the family, and states their relationship to himself. However, careful reading will often yield more than this. You should pay attention to clauses like 'when he reaches the age of . .', which indicates that the person concerned had not reached that age at the time the will was written. Similarly, anything which refers to a person as being unmarried, but whom you know to have married at some later date, might help you to narrow the range of a marriage search. If it is clear from the will that they are already married, then you will know that the marriage must have taken place before the date of the will. In the case of women, this information is often implied, by the surname used. Reference may also be made to persons who died before the testator made the will. For example, nieces or nephews may be described as 'the children of my deceased brother, Charles'. This would place the date of the said brother's death before the date of the will, and if they are also shown as being under a particular age, then that would help place an earlier limit on their father's death. There are some assumptions which you should avoid. The first is that a man's wife is the mother of any or all of his children. In the past, re-marriage because of the death of a spouse was as common as is re-marriage following divorce today. Other false assumptions are that all of a person's children must be named in their will, or that their omission means that they were out of favour. Similarly, a very small legacy to one child — the proverbial 'cut off with a shilling' — does not automatically mean that they were being slighted by their parent. It could be that the eldest son had already taken over the running of the family business, and was receiving the profits from it, or a daughter had been given her portion when she married. A helpful testator might explain his reasons for this, but equally might not. With almost every record source you consult in your research, you should bear in mind that it was created for a particular purpose at the time, and not for the instruction and entertainment of future generations of family historians. The writer of a will might have more of an eye on posterity than most, but their main purpose was still to make clear their instructions for the disposal of the estate. Occasionally you may find a testator who gives a great deal of detail about their family. Isaac Merritt Singer, inventor of the Singer Sewing Machine, was an American, but he spent the last years of his life in

England, where he died in 1875. His will runs to twelve pages, and in it he names his eight sons, thirteen daughters, the husbands of three married daughters, his wife and both her parents. Six of his children were by his wife, the rest were by four other women, all of whom he names. One of these women was commonly known by a different surname from her official one, which he also gives. In addition, he gives his wife's date and place of birth, the date and place of their marriage, including his wife's surname at that time, which was not her surname at birth, and the name of the clergyman who performed the ceremony. One of his daughters receives nothing in the will, but he helpfully explains that this is because her husband occupies a position in the Singer Manufacturing Company 'and has thus acquired a fortune which places my said daughter above the necessity of any assistance from me'. You will be unusually fortunate if you find all of these kinds of detail in a will, but you may find one or two of them.

Finally, there are occasional personal touches, which obviously come from the heart, and stand out from the standard legal language around them. A greengrocer who died in 1924 left small sums to several members of his family, including £10 to his youngest brother 'for a new barrow to be built by Mr Hales, East Street Sittingbourne'. More colourfully, a bookseller in Cambridge in the late 19th century left his house to his wife and children, on condition that they only lived in it themselves, and did not rent it to students 'for undergraduate lodgers are more like hogs and wolves than human beings'. These are timely reminders that, although they are serious legal documents, wills are made by living, breathing individuals with thoughts and feelings, and sometimes scores to settle, like the man who left his wife 'the box she broke open when she nearly murdered me and the hatchet she tried to burn and which I recovered by the aid of the policeman'.

Women and wills

It has already been noted that relatively few wills were made by women, but they appear frequently as beneficiaries, and those wills which were made by women can be of great interest. The legal disadvantages suffered by women before the Married Women's Property Act also had effects beyond the fact that married women could not make wills. As anything owned by a woman automatically became the property of her husband when she married, this was often borne in mind by those who left a legacy to a woman. If a man left money to his daughters, he might include a clause such as 'for her sole and separate use benefit and behoof for ever free from the debts control or interference of her present or any future husband she may have'. The bequests to Isaac Singer's daughters all contain this clause. This does not mean that a testator disliked his son-in-law. His daughter might have been a young child at the time he made the will, and his intention would be to protect her inheritance against all future eventualities.

Similarly, he might leave his wife only an income which would cease if she re-married. If they had children, this could be a way of protecting their interests. A young widow would be very likely to re-marry, and if her first husband left her a substantial sum absolutely, this would pass to her new husband, who would not necessarily have the interests of his step-children at heart. If a man left the bulk of his estate in trust for his children until they were of age, with an income for his widow during her widowhood, then the interests of all his dependents were protected. It does not necessarily mean that he wanted to prevent his widow ever re-marrying. Some women were of course in a position to make wills in their own right, even before the Married Women's Property Act came into force. Widows and spinsters could leave wills, if they had anything to leave, and these can be very informative. Childless widows who had been left substantial sums by their husbands would be in a position to leave something to other members of the family, or to friends, and some spinsters would also be able to do this. Neither of these will usually be anyone's direct ancestor, but their wills are likely to mention their brothers, sisters, nieces and nephews. You should not therefore neglect the wills of sisters and aunts, some of whom will have different surnames from your direct ancestors.

Grants of probate

Wills can be fascinating and informative documents, and it is easy to overlook the fact that for every will there is also an accompanying Grant of Probate. This may give no more information than is shown in the index, but sometimes contains more, particularly when the grant is made a long time after the date of death. The grant gives the addresses and sometimes occupations of the executors, and their relationship, if any, to the testator, details which may not be in the will itself.

Intestacy

A person who dies without leaving a will is said to be 'intestate'. If there is property to be dealt with, the widow or next of kin can apply for a Grant of Letters of Administration so that the estate can be distributed, according to a set formula. This has varied over the years, and also depends on the number and closeness of the surviving relatives. Real estate and personal estate were dealt with differently up to 1926. ***Whitaker's Almanack*** always gives the rules for the current year, so the volume for the year in which a grant was made will indicate how the estate might have been split among the deceased person's family. In general, if a man left a widow and legitimate children, the estate would be split between them. A married woman's estate would go to her husband, and that of a bachelor or spinster would go to their parents, or be shared between their brothers and sisters if the parents were dead. As with Grants of Probate, a Grant of Letters of Administration will often give no more information than appears in the index, but it is worth the very small cost just in case there is additional detail, which might prove invaluable.

Searching in the indexes

The indexes, properly called calendars, are in annual volumes from 1858 right up to the current year. Wills and administrations are listed separately until 1870, but from 1871 are listed together, in one alphabetical sequence, which makes searching quicker. The calendars for the most recent years are made available on microfiche to begin with, but are eventually bound into books. The only exception to this is 1995, where the original computer file has been lost, so the microfiche calendars will remain the only ones available. In future, the most recent calendars will be accessible on computer terminals in the search room at First Avenue House. The early calendars are the most detailed, giving the full name and address of the deceased, the date and place of death, the date and place of probate or grant of administration, the names and addresses of the executors or administrators, and their relationship, if any, to the deceased. There will also be an indication of the value of the estate. Occupations may also be given, and the marital status of a woman will be shown, often with the name of her husband if he is still alive. All these details appear in the calendars from 1858 to 1891. From 1892 the addresses and relationships of executors and administrators no longer appear, and from 1958 the names of husbands are not shown. From 1968 to the present, only the name, address and date of death of the deceased, the date and place of probate or administration and the value of the estate are given. The full name is always given, with any other name by which they were known, and cross-referenced if necessary. This is usually no more dramatic than a minor difference in spelling, or a middle name which was not always used, but occasionally a genuine alias will be revealed. You may be able to go straight to a census search from an address in the calendar, particularly if your ancestor died close to a census date. The place of probate will be London (the Principal Registry) or one of the District Registries. Executors and administrators would have used the Registry most convenient for them, which will often be the one closest to the deceased's normal residence. During the Second World War, the Principal Probate Registry was moved out of London to Llandudno, so wills and grants made there do not imply a hitherto unsuspected family connection with North Wales.

Additional documents

Occasionally there may be additional material relating to a particular case. If a will refers to other documents, it is worth asking if they have been kept on file. There is relatively little of this at First Avenue House, but if a will was proved at a District Registry, they or the appropriate Record Office may have kept the relevant papers. If a calendar entry includes the words 'former grant cessate' or 'by decree', this indicates that there was a dispute over the estate, and you should be able to see a copy of the judgement. This will not include any of the evidence, but you may be able to find the records of the court case from this information, and perhaps even newspaper reports. The Public Record Office at Kew holds a 7% sample of Contentious Probate Case Files in class J121, just over 9000 cases. They are indexed alphabetically, by year.

Death Duty Registers

Death Duty, or Estate Duty, Registers cover the period 1796-1903. They are of most use before 1858, when their indexes are the nearest equivalent to a national probate index, but can still be useful for the later period in some circumstances. While a will shows a testator's intentions, the Estate Duty Register shows how the estate was actually distributed. This is of particular interest in cases of intestacy, where there is no will and therefore no clues as to distribution. Where a testator left legacies in the form of annuities, trusts and life interests, it may be possible to follow the fortunes of his heirs over many years. However, these records can be very difficult to interpret, and there are a number of missing or incomplete entries. The annual indexes are on microfilm (IR 27) at the Family Records Centre and the Public Record Office at Kew. The registers (IR 26) after 1858 have not been filmed, and can only be consulted at Kew, where three days notice is required for their production. For a detailed account of these records, see Jane Cox's two books *Introduction to Wills Probate & Death Duty Records; Affection Defying the Power of Death* and *Wills, Inventories and Death Duties.* The second of these is out of print, but should be available in libraries.

Reading and copying

Access to the calendars is free, but a small fee is payable if you want to look at a will or grant, or to order a photocopy, or both. Currently this is 25p to read a will or grant, 25p for a copy of a grant, and 75p for a copy of a will, regardless of the number of pages. You can read a will on the same day, provided it is ordered and paid for by 3pm. Copies can be ready for collection in the search room, or posted to you, about a week after your visit. There is no extra charge for postage. Having found an entry relating to your ancestor, you can decide to read the will or grant that day, or order a photocopy. As the copy wills are held in a different building, it takes about an hour before a copy is available for you to read. You may not remove this copy from the search room. Whether you want to read or order a copy of a will or grant, you must complete an application form, giving the full name of the deceased, and the date and registry of probate. For wills proved before 1931 in London (the Principal Registry) a folio number is also required. This is a handwritten number in the margin of the calendar. Tick the boxes indicating whether the document is a will or a grant, and to show whether you want to read it or order a copy, and then fill in your name and address. Each application must be on a separate form, so if you want both a will and its accompanying grant, you must complete two forms. This is because the two kinds of document are held in different parts of the archive. When you have done this, take the completed form and the calendar book to the desk for checking. There is no need to take the microfiche if you are using a recent calendar, as the clerk has a duplicate set. You may take two books up at a time, but no more. When the clerk has checked and signed the form, return the calendar to its shelf, take the form to the cashier's window, and pay the appropriate fee. Payments may be in cash, or cheque with a cheque card (payable to Her Majesty's Paymaster General). Debit cards, credit cards and travellers cheques are not accepted. If you are likely to order several copies, it makes sense to save them up and pay for them all together, but for reading it is advisable to pay as you go. Return your applications to the counter, where you will be given an envelope to address for copies to be posted, or advised about when they will be ready if you have chosen to collect them. If you have ordered a copy to read, an officer will call your name when it is ready, in about an hour. You may then collect the copy and read it at one of the tables provided. You may take notes, but full transcription is not allowed. If you then decide to order a copy, tell the officer when you return it to the desk, when your application form will be returned to you, so that you can pay the fee for copying, as already described.

Calendars held elsewhere.
First Avenue House holds the only complete set of calendars from 1858 to date, but there are numerous sets of calendars covering shorter periods elsewhere. District Probate Registries will usually have them for about the last 50 years, and some record offices may also have a set from 1858 to 1930 or 1943, possibly on microfiche or microfilm. There are sets in London at the Family Records Centre and the Guildhall Library (both on microfiche, up to 1943) and at the Society of Genealogists (microfilm, up to 1930). The set at the Family Records Centre is particularly convenient if you want to find an address to search in the census. For further details, see ***Probate Jurisdictions: Where To Look For Wills.*** Although all of these are copies of the original calendar books, they do not include any handwritten additions, so they do not have the folio numbers for London-registered wills before 1931. This means that if you find a reference to one of these on a microfilm or microfiche calendar, you must remember to add the folio number from the calendar if you subsequently visit First Avenue House to read it or order a copy. As well as folio numbers, other additions are sometimes

made to the calendars, when there is a further grant of probate, or when the original value of the estate is re-calculated (resworn). A further grant of probate may be made some years after the original one, and will appear in the calendar for that year, with a reference to the original grant. If you find such an entry, the will is stored in the year of the first grant of probate, and each grant will be in its respective year.

Multiple Applications

Although most people will want to read or order only a few wills or grants, there are those who require large numbers of them, for instance if they are doing a One-Name Study. No more than 40 items may be ordered by one person on the same day. When you order a lot of documents, one of the most time-consuming aspects is taking the calendars to the desk for checking. Regular users can apply for a special pass, which entitles them to complete the forms and take them directly to the cashier, without checking. If you would like such a pass, you should enquire at the desk. You will need to sign a declaration to the effect that the correct completion of the form is your responsibility, and it is your loss if the will or grant cannot be produced because the form is incorrect or incomplete. As the sums involved are small, and the time saved is potentially great, most regular users will be happy with this arrangement. One or two careless mistakes can concentrate the mind wonderfully.

Orders by post

If you are unable to visit First Avenue House, or the appropriate District Probate Registry, you can order by post by writing to:

The Postal Searches and Copies Department
The Probate Registry
Duncombe Place
York YO1 2EA   Phone/Fax: 01904-624210

For a fee, currently £2, they will provide a copy of a will or grant. The fee includes a search of up to 3 years. You must provide the full name, date of death and last known address. If you are unsure of the date of death, they will conduct a search for you at the rate of £2 for each three-year period if you specify the year in which you would like the search to start. As with personal applications, cheques should be made payable to HMPG.

If you require a more specialized search, you may prefer to use a record agent. An example of this type of search might be if you wanted copies of all the wills and grants for a particular surname within a specified period, or a list of all such entries from which you could then choose which to order. Many record agents advertise in *Family Tree Magazine* and other journals.

USEFUL ADDRESSES

British Library, Oriental and India Office Collections, 96 Euston Road, St Pancras, London NW1 2DB
Family Records Centre, 1 Myddelton Street, Islington, London EC1R 1UW
Guildhall Library, Aldermanbury, London EC2P 2EJ
National Archives, Bishop Street, Dublin 8, Republic of Ireland
Postal Searches and Copies Department, The Probate Registry, Duncombe Place, York YO1 2EA
Public Record Office, Kew, Surrey TW9 4DU
Public Record Office of Northern Ireland, 66 Balmoral Avenue, Belfast BT9 6NY
Scottish Record Office, General Register House, Edinburgh EH1 3YY
Society of Genealogists, 14 Charterhouse Buildings, Goswell Road, London EC1M 7BA

BIBLIOGRAPHY

Cox, Jane, *Introduction to Wills Probate & Death Duty Records; Affection Defying the Power of Death* FFHS 1993
Cox, Jane *Wills, Inventories and Death Duties* PRO 1988
Gibson, Jeremy, *Probate Jurisdictions: Where To Look For Wills* 4th edn. FFHS 1997
Genealogical Services Directory GR Specialist Information Services 1998